# Bits and Pieces

Start collecting bits and pieces to make the wonderful pictures in this book. You'll need paper and card, wool and felt, sequins and beads, foil, glitter and paints, sponge and fancy sweet wrappers.

You can either make the pictures just the same as the ones in the book, or you can use the ideas to design your own. There are all sorts of exciting and unusual painting techniques for you to try out as well.

## Acknowledgements

Designed by **Jane Warring**
Illustrations by **Lindy Norton**
Pictures made by **Karen Radford**
Photographs by **Peter Millard**
Created by **Thumbprint Books**

First published in hardback in 1995,
first published in paperback in 1995
by Hamlyn Children's Books
an imprint of Reed Children's Books
Michelin House, 81 Fulham Road
London SW3 6RB

Hardback ISBN 0600 584763
Paperback ISBN 0600 586170

Printed and bound in Belgium by Proost

# Making Pictures
# SPOOKY THINGS

Penny King and Clare Roundhill

# Contents

HAMLYN

# Grinning Ghosts

Create this picture of a family of ghosts gliding across a starry sky. Add extra special stars made from yellow card stuck on to tiny pieces of sponge. Decorate the ghosts with sparkling red eyes, grinning mouths and silver glitter.

## Bits and Pieces

- White card
- White candle
- Paints & brush
- Scissors & glue
- White crêpe paper
- Cotton wool balls
- White thread
- Glitter
- Black felt pen
- Yellow card
- Bits of sponge

Draw little stars all over the white card, using the end of a white candle. Press down hard.

Paint over the stars with watery dark blue paint (see paint tip). Leave the paint to dry.

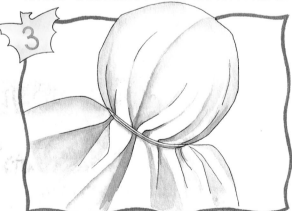

Put a ball of cotton wool in the centre of a white crêpe square. Tie it in place with white thread.

Add red glitter eyes, black mouths and silver glitter to each ghost. Stick them on the sky.

# A Haunted Wood

Create a creepy crêpe haunted wood swarming with spooky creatures.

Give it a misty, eerie look by gluing a thin layer of cotton wool over the trees.

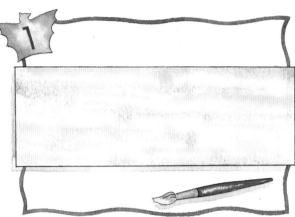

Paint a misty background on a long piece of white card or stiff paper (see paint tip).

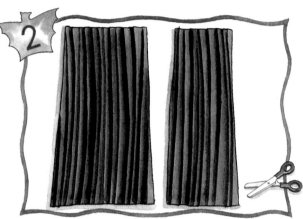

Cut thick tree trunks from black crêpe paper with the wrinkles going from top to bottom.

**PAINT TIP**
Brush water all over the piece of stiff white card until it is quite wet. Using a fat brush, paint thick streaks of pale grey, blue and pink across the paper. Let it dry.

**3**

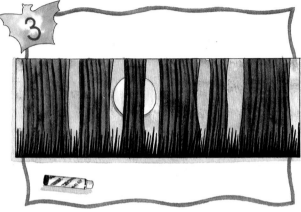

**4**

Glue a big silver moon and the wrinkly tree trunks on to the sky. Add spiky crêpe paper grass.

Cut spooky eyes out of shiny card. Glue them on the trees. Add a layer of cottonwool mist.

# A Mad Monster

Let your imagination go wild when you make this mad monster picture. Give him eyes that stick out on stalks, big ears, a spotty nose and a huge tongue. Make a mad pipe-cleaner spider with beady eyes to stick in his hideous hair.

**Bits and Pieces**
- Lid of a box
- Paints & brush
- Sponges
- Scissors & glue
- Black card
- Felt
- 2 corks
- Silver foil
- Black wool
- Pipe-cleaners
- 2 small beads
- Red card

**1** Paint the lid (see paint tip). Cut out sponge ears, a tongue and nose. Paint spots on the nose.

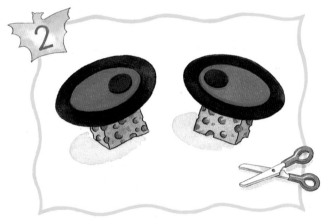

**2** Glue red felt eyes on to circles of card. Cut two bits of sponge. Glue the eyes on to them.

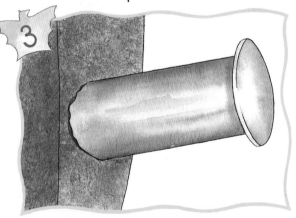

**3** Cover two corks with foil. Glue foil circles on top. Cut holes in the lid and push in the corks.

**4** Glue the eyes, ears, tongue, nose and wool hair on to the head. Stick it on the red card.

**PAINT TIP**
Make different shades of
green using blue, yellow and
green paint. Dab the paint
all over the box lid with a
piece of sponge. Overlap
the shades while the paint is
wet to give a blotchy effect.

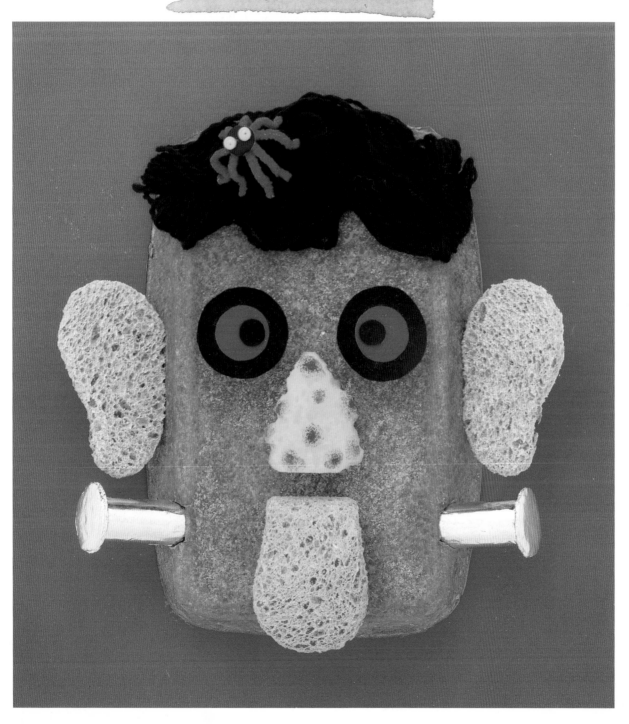

# A Scaredy Cat

This cat is frightened of the streaks of lightning flashing across the sky. Look how her back arches and her hair stands on end! Make the lightning really glow by spreading zigzags of glue on the paper. Then sprinkle them with glitter.

**Bits and Pieces**

- Stiff white paper
- Scissors
- Black, grey & white paint
- Paintbrush
- PVA glue
- Silver & gold glitter
- Green card
- Black pipe-cleaners
- Shiny card

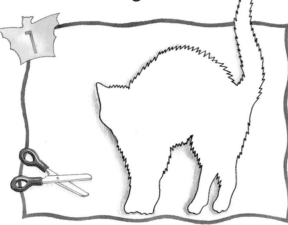

Draw the outline of a cat with an arched back and upright tail on white paper. Cut it out.

Paint the cat with zigzags of black, grey and white paint mixed with PVA (see paint tip).

Before the paint dries, sprinkle silver glitter all over the cat. Glue the cat on to green card.

Paint a nose and mouth. Glue on pipe-cleaner whiskers, card eyes and claws. Add lightning.

12

**PAINT TIP**
For the cat's stripes, mix an
equal amount of black paint
with some PVA glue. Do the
same with some grey and
some white paint. The PVA
glue makes the glitter stick
to the wet paint.

13

# A Mysterious Mirror

In this picture, a ghostly creature appears to loom out of an ancient mirror, which hangs above a hot, roaring fire. To make the creature look mysterious, give him red eyes that glint in the dark and long, claw-like silver fingers.

**Bits and Pieces**
- White paper
- Paint
- Two small pots
- Drinking straw
- Wrapping paper
- Black card
- Scissors & glue
- Black crêpe paper
- Coloured card
- Silver foil
- Red glitter

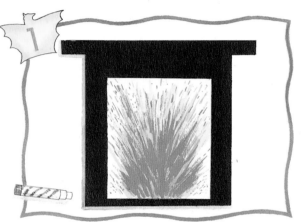

**1** Paint a fire on white paper (see paint tip). Glue it on to a black card fireplace, like this.

**2** Glue the fireplace on to the wrapping paper. Stick on crumpled black crêpe coal.

**3** Glue a brown card oval to the wrapping paper. Glue a smaller silver oval on top for a mirror.

**4** Mould a foil face and hands. Glue them on the mirror. Add card candles and candlesticks.

# A Moaning Mummy

Make this ghostly picture of a mummy slowly rising from its deep, dark tomb.

Give it large, sunken black eyes with big, silver glitter pupils, and a sad mouth.

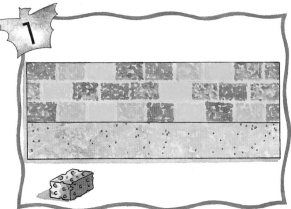

Sponge a brick pattern on to the yellow card (see paint tip). Glue couscous on the bottom.

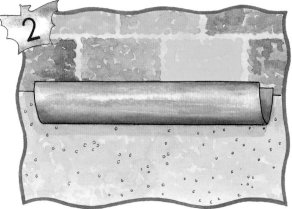

Cut the cardboard tube in half along its length. Cover it in silver foil. Stick it on the couscous.

**PAINT TIP**

Cut a small rectangle out of a sponge. Soak it in water and then squeeze it dry. Press it in orange paint. Print rows of bricks along the top half of the yellow card, leaving a space between each one. Let the paint dry before you stick couscous on the bottom half.

## Bits and Pieces

- Yellow card
- Paint
- Cellulose sponge
- Glue & scissors
- Couscous
- Cardboard tube
- Silver foil
- White card
- White loo paper
- Black paper
- Shiny paper
- Silver glitter

Cut out a card head, hand and foot. Wrap them with loo paper. Add a mouth and eyes.

Glue the mummy on to the tomb, like this. Stick shiny paper creepy crawlies all around it.

17

# A Shaking Skeleton

You'll need different kinds and shapes of pasta to make this smiling, shaking skeleton. If you want to make him extra spooky, paint the pasta fluorescent colours before you stick them down so that he shines in the dark.

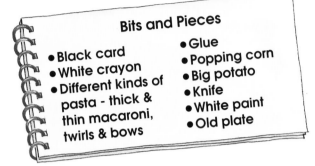

**Bits and Pieces**

- Black card
- White crayon
- Different kinds of pasta - thick & thin macaroni, twirls & bows
- Glue
- Popping corn
- Big potato
- Knife
- White paint
- Old plate

Lightly draw a skeleton in white crayon on black card. Choose pasta shapes for all the bones.

Stick down the pasta shapes for the spine, ribs, pelvis and shoulder blades, as shown.

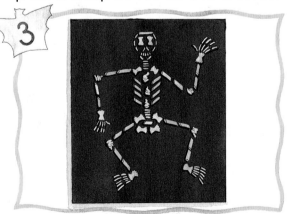

Add pasta arms, legs, hands, fingers, toes and a skull. Use pop corn for his smiley teeth.

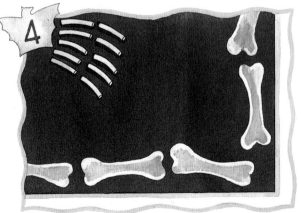

Print a border of white bones all around the edge of the black paper (see paint tip).

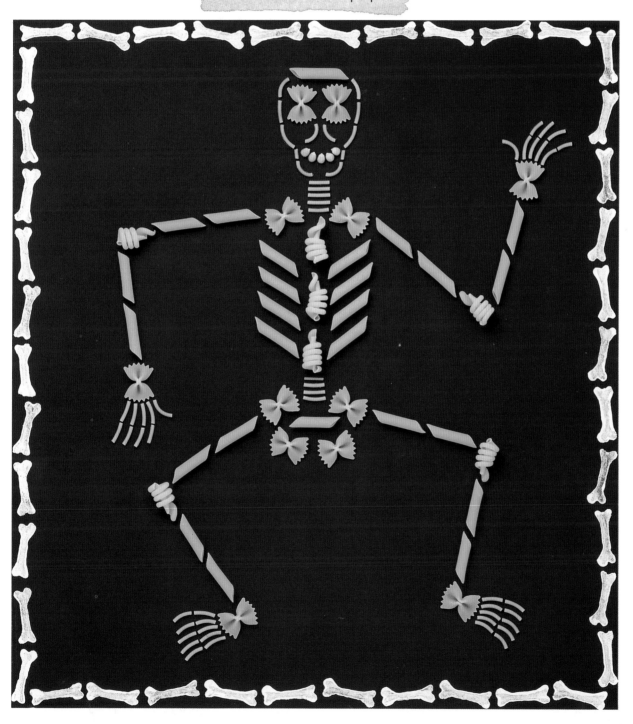

19

# A Spooky Sky

Make a night sky picture with stars, moons and colourful paper bats to stick on a window. In the day, light will shine through the tissue paper and make the bats and stars really stand out. At night, the sky will turn a deep, dark blue.

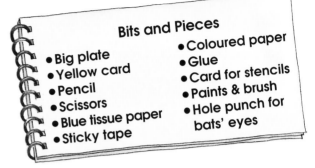

**Bits and Pieces**
- Big plate
- Yellow card
- Pencil
- Scissors
- Blue tissue paper
- Sticky tape
- Coloured paper
- Glue
- Card for stencils
- Paints & brush
- Hole punch for bats' eyes

Draw around a big plate in the centre of the yellow card to make a big circle. Cut it out.

Tape a large piece of dark blue tissue paper across the back of the hole in the card.

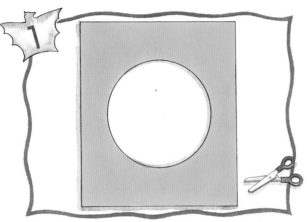

Cut out bats and stars from coloured paper. Carefully glue them on to the tissue sky.

Stencil bats, stars and moons all around the edges of the yellow card (see paint tip).

# A Horrible Hand

Here's a truly horrible, hairy hand picture. The easiest way to make it is to draw around an adult's hand on to some paper. Make the fingers longer than they really are. Print a potato-cut border of scary, smiling skulls.

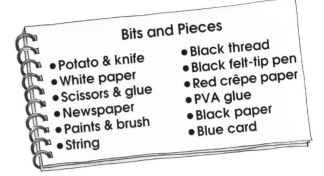

**Bits and Pieces**
- Potato & knife
- White paper
- Scissors & glue
- Newspaper
- Paints & brush
- String
- Black thread
- Black felt-tip pen
- Red crêpe paper
- PVA glue
- Black paper
- Blue card

**1** Cut out a paper hand with long fingers. Glue rolled-up newspaper on it, as shown.

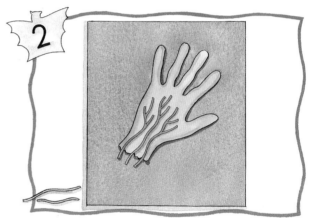

**2** Turn the hand over and paint it. Stick it on the blue card. Glue on blue painted string veins.

**3** Dab glue on the wrist and fingers. Press on black thread for hair. Paint black knuckles.

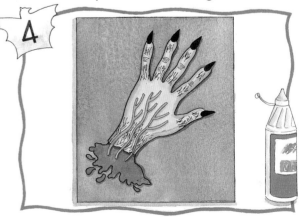

**4** Make some blood (see paint tip). Dab it under the wrist. Add shiny black paper nails.

**PAINT TIP**
To make a gooey blood mixture, mix an equal amount of red paint with some PVA glue in an old saucer. Stir in some strips of red crêpe paper to make the blood look extra thick.

23

# A Wicked Witch

Draw a big, ugly old witch with a dress, cloak and pointed hat on some paper. Then use the outlines to cut out a card head and hands and felt clothes and give her long, straggly, sparkly hair. Let her streak across the sky on her broomstick.

**Bits and Pieces**

- Pencil & paper
- Felt & scissors
- Striped fabric
- White card
- Paint & brush
- PVA glue
- Sawdust
- Twigs and string
- Purple card
- Sticky stars
- Lace & ric-rac
- Tinsel or wool

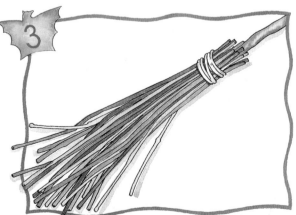

Cut out a felt hat, cloak and dress. Glue felt stars and moons on the dress. Cut out two legs.

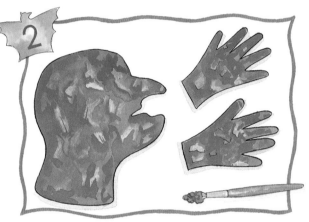

Draw a witch's face and hands on white paper. Cut them out and paint them (see paint tip).

Use string to bind a bunch of thin twigs around a long stick to make a witch's broomstick.

Stick everything on the purple card. Add sticky stars. Glue on a petticoat, ric-rac and hair.

# Peculiar Pumpkins

Here's a magical way of making a pumpkin picture or poster for Hallowe'en.

Watch their grisly, grinning faces appear as you wash away the white paint.

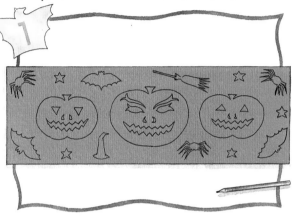

Draw three grinning pumpkin faces on the orange card with a border of creepy shapes.

Brush white paint over the pumpkins and creepy shapes (see paint tip). Let them dry.

## Bits and Pieces

- Pencil
- Long sheet of stiff orange paper or card
- White paint
- Thin paintbrush
- Thick paintbrush
- Old saucer
- Black Indian ink or waterproof ink
- Running water
- Sponge

**PAINT TIP**
Paint a thin layer of white paint over the parts of the picture you want to keep the same colour as the card. You can use any colour ink or card you like.

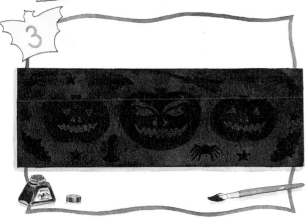

Cover the whole picture with black Indian ink, using a thick brush. Let the ink dry.

Hold the picture under a tap. Gently rub off the white paint with a sponge. Let the card dry.

27

# A Creepy Castle

Make skeletons and a green hand to haunt this creepy castle. Ask an adult to help you cut out the windows and a door that opens. Add a pipe-cleaner chandelier, cotton wool cobwebs and ghosts lurking behind the windows.

## Bits and Pieces

- Shoebox
- Scalpel or knife
- Paints, brush & fine rag
- Cellophane
- Yoghurt pots
- Fabric & trim
- Scissors & glue
- Card & pictures
- Crêpe paper
- Black thread
- Pipe-cleaners

Paint the box (see paint tip). Paint the door and cover the windows with cellophane.

Cut pictures from magazines. Glue them on gold card frames and stick them on the walls.

Cut a chair and stool out of yoghurt pots. Stick fabric over them. Add fancy trimmings.

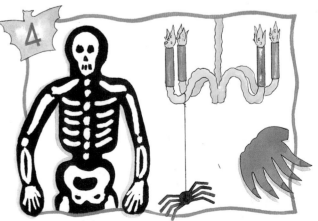

Make painted crêpe skeletons, a hand and a chandelier with a dangling spider. Fix in place.

28

29

Fast Movers

# THE REALLY
# HAIRY
# SCARY
# SPIDER

Spiders
Galore

## AND OTHER CREATURES
## WITH LOTS OF LEGS

## THERESA GREENAWAY

Hairy Hunters

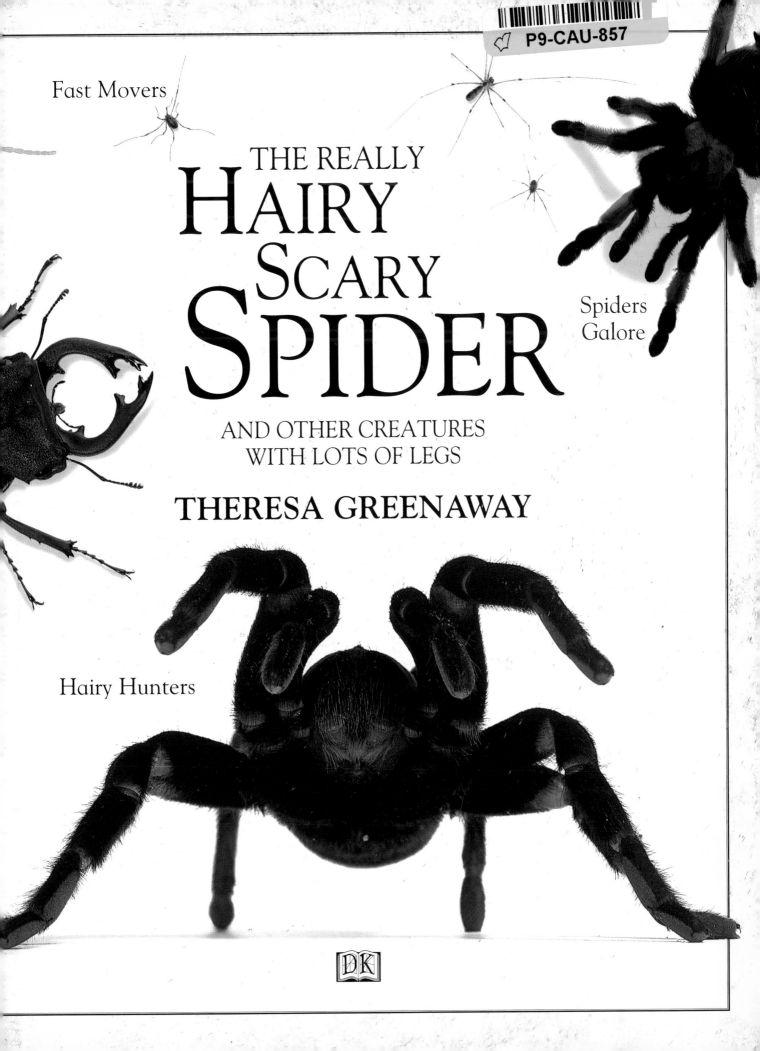

DK

# SPIDERS GALORE

What is it about spiders that makes us shiver? Is it their hairy bodies, their long legs, or their sticky webs? While these are the features that make them successful hunters, most spiders are unable to give us so much as a harmless nip.

Jumping spider

Leaf-mimicking spider

This spider disguises itself as a piece of dead leaf so that prey won't notice it.

Huntsman spider

The deadly funnel-web spider will attack anything that accidentally get in its way. It moves, even people.

House spiders actually help us by ridding our homes of insect pests.

House spider

Funnel-web spider

Harvestman

To protect themselves, many spiders paralyze struggling victims with a poisoned bite before tieing them up with strong silk threads.

Tarantula

Daddy-long-legs spider

Tarantulas are sometimes so big their legs can span a dinner plate.

Tarantula

Large spiders, such as this tarantula, can eat frogs, lizards, and even snakes.

# HAIRY HUNTERS

Some of the biggest, hairiest spiders of all are actually pretty timid. A tarantula would only ever sink its huge fangs into a person in self-defense.

Even though tarantulas have huge bodies, they have very small venom glands.

Tarantula

In spite of having up to eight eyes, most hairy spiders have poor eyesight.

Tarantula

When threatened, tarantulas flick hairs that itch and sting into their enemies faces.

Tarantula

Once a year, a tarantula sheds its skin. When this happens, any hairs lost over the last year are replaced.

Huntsman spiders

Huntsman spiders will eat cockroaches.

Some female tarantulas have been known to live for up to 30 years.

Tarantula

A trapdoor spider lives in a silk-lined tunnel. It peeks out of the slightly open trapdoor lid, waiting to seize any passing insects.

An untreated funnel-web bite is deadly. Fortunately, an antivenin now saves most victims.

Funnel-web spider

A funnel-web's knife-sharp fangs can easily pierce fingernail or bone.

Trapdoor spider

Tarantulas' fangs aren't very venomous. Instead, these spiders crush prey and then cover them in digestive juices.

Sensitive hairs on its legs warn this spider of approaching danger – or dinner.

Tarantula

A tarantula is a slow eater. It will usually drag prey back to its burrow before eating it.

# FAST MOVERS

We're often startled when a spindly spider suddenly appears, darting up a wall or scuttling across a floor. But, while it may be running very fast, it's probably running away from us.

Harvestman

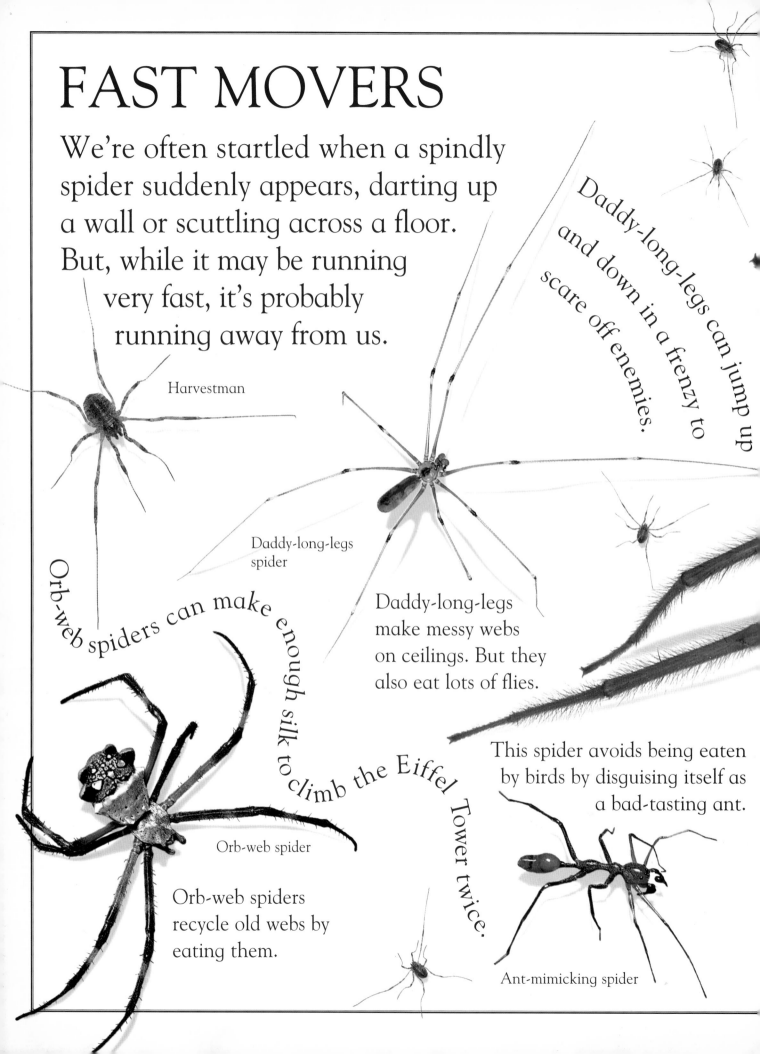

Daddy-long-legs can jump up and down in a frenzy to scare off enemies.

Daddy-long-legs spider

Daddy-long-legs make messy webs on ceilings. But they also eat lots of flies.

Orb-web spiders can make enough silk to climb the Eiffel Tower twice.

Orb-web spider

Orb-web spiders recycle old webs by eating them.

This spider avoids being eaten by birds by disguising itself as a bad-tasting ant.

Ant-mimicking spider

Orb-web spider

Experts can identify a species of orb-web spider just by looking at the shape of its web.

A house spider could scare you by rushing out from under your chair. But it's not after your toes, it's just afraid you'll move and squash it!

*Spider silk is one of the strongest and lightest of all known fibers.*

A harvestman isn't a spider. Unlike true spiders, it doesn't have a separate head and body.

Harvestman

House spider

House spiders don't climb up pipes, as many people think. If you find one in your tub or sink, it probably just slipped in and couldn't get back out.

Jumping spiders can leap 40 times their body length. That's like a child jumping an Olympic swimming pool.

Jumping spider

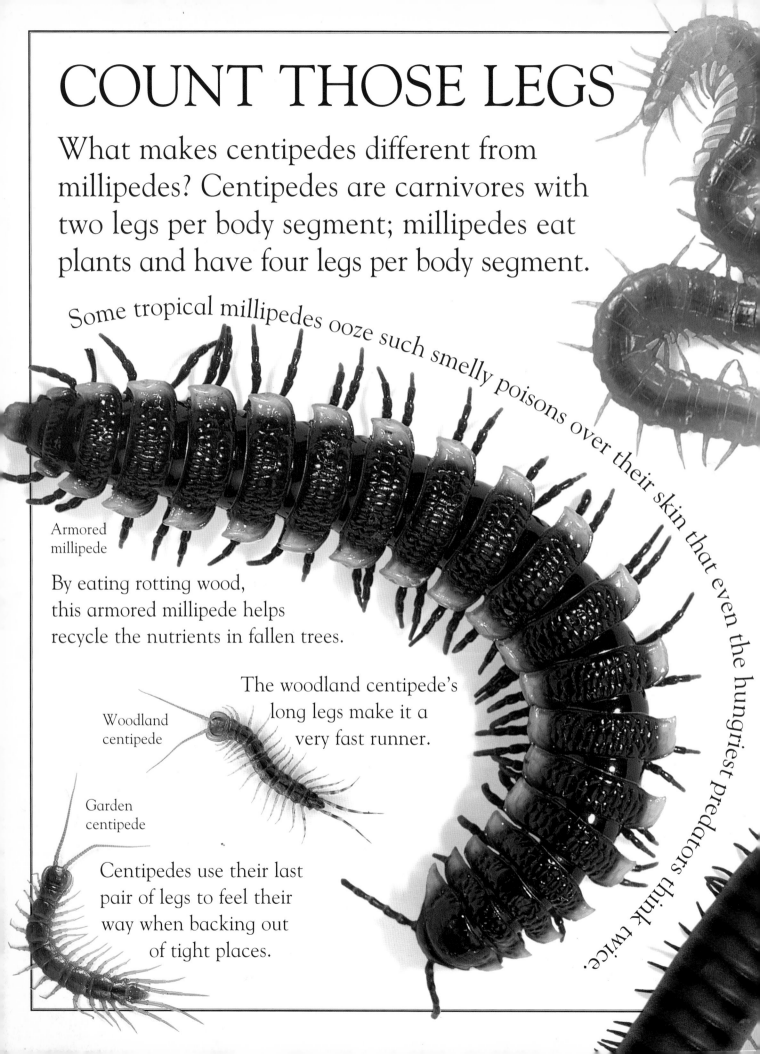

# COUNT THOSE LEGS

What makes centipedes different from millipedes? Centipedes are carnivores with two legs per body segment; millipedes eat plants and have four legs per body segment.

Some tropical millipedes ooze such smelly poisons over their skin that even the hungriest predators think twice.

Armored millipede

By eating rotting wood, this armored millipede helps recycle the nutrients in fallen trees.

The woodland centipede's long legs make it a very fast runner.

Woodland centipede

Garden centipede

Centipedes use their last pair of legs to feel their way when backing out of tight places.

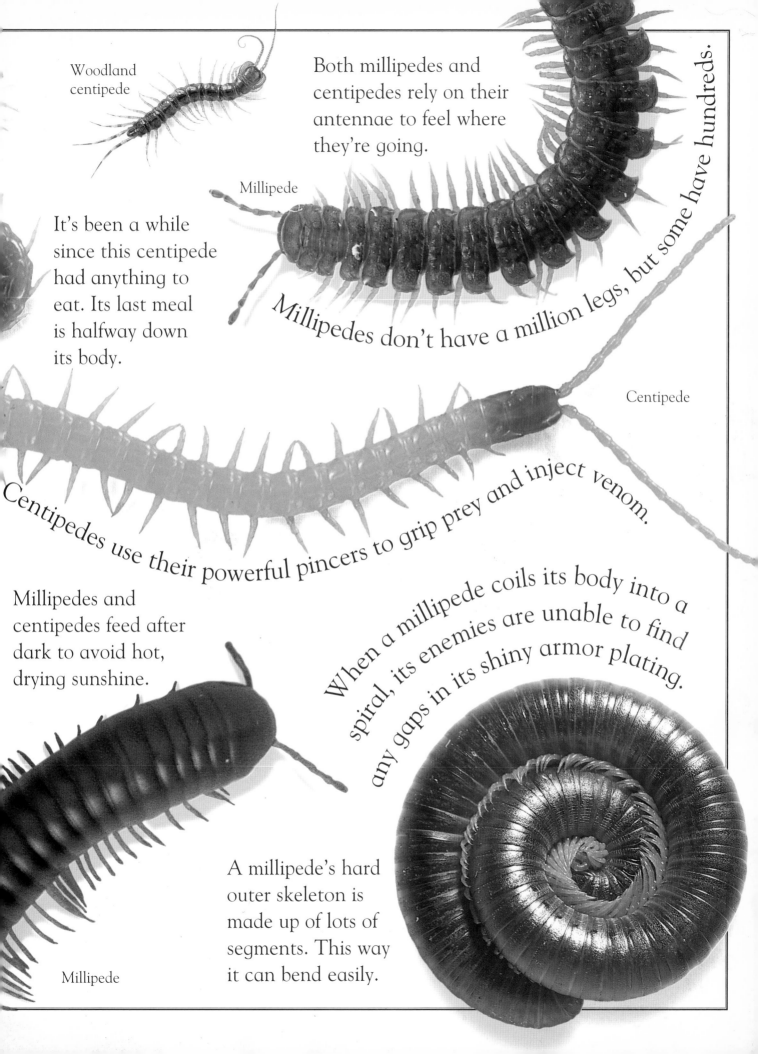

Woodland centipede

Both millipedes and centipedes rely on their antennae to feel where they're going.

Millipede

It's been a while since this centipede had anything to eat. Its last meal is halfway down its body.

Millipedes don't have a million legs, but some have hundreds.

Centipede

Centipedes use their powerful pincers to grip prey and inject venom.

Millipedes and centipedes feed after dark to avoid hot, drying sunshine.

When a millipede coils its body into a spiral, its enemies are unable to find any gaps in its shiny armor plating.

A millipede's hard outer skeleton is made up of lots of segments. This way it can bend easily.

Millipede

# CLEVER DISGUISES

Many animals use camouflage to escape the sharp eyes of predators. Stick and leaf insects are real experts. They sit, motionless, looking just like parts of plants. You may not see them, but they'll see you.

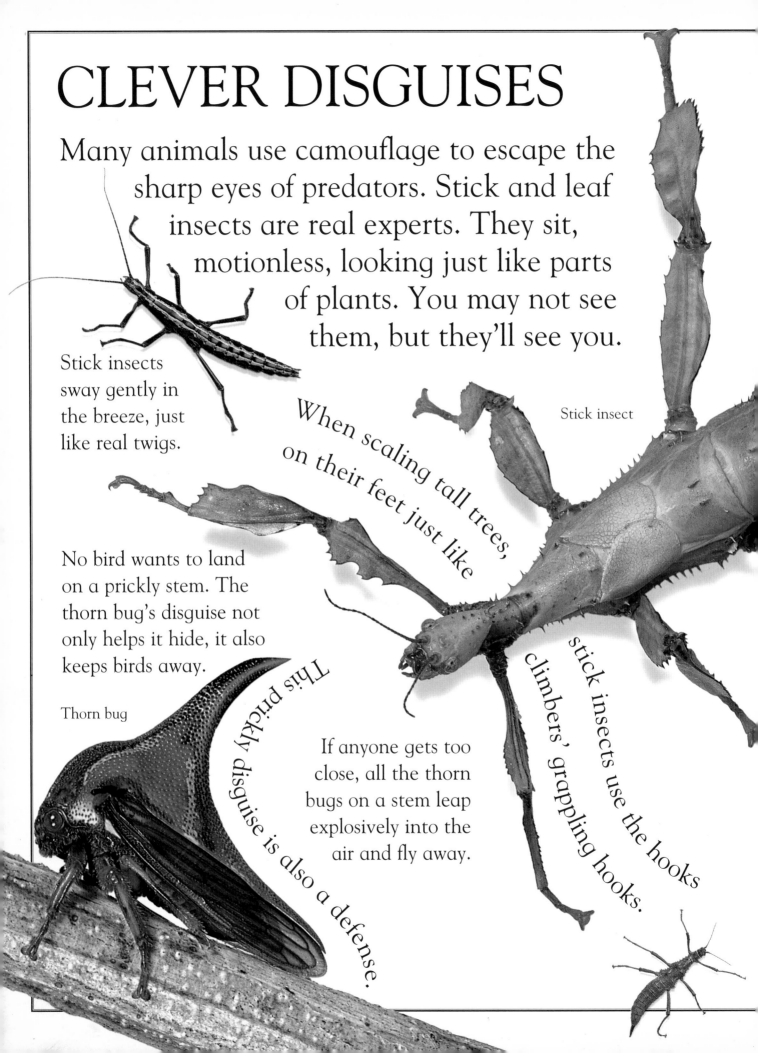

Stick insects sway gently in the breeze, just like real twigs.

Stick insect

When scaling tall trees, on their feet just like

No bird wants to land on a prickly stem. The thorn bug's disguise not only helps it hide, it also keeps birds away.

Thorn bug

This prickly disguise is also a defense.

stick insects use the hooks climbers' grappling hooks.

If anyone gets too close, all the thorn bugs on a stem leap explosively into the air and fly away.

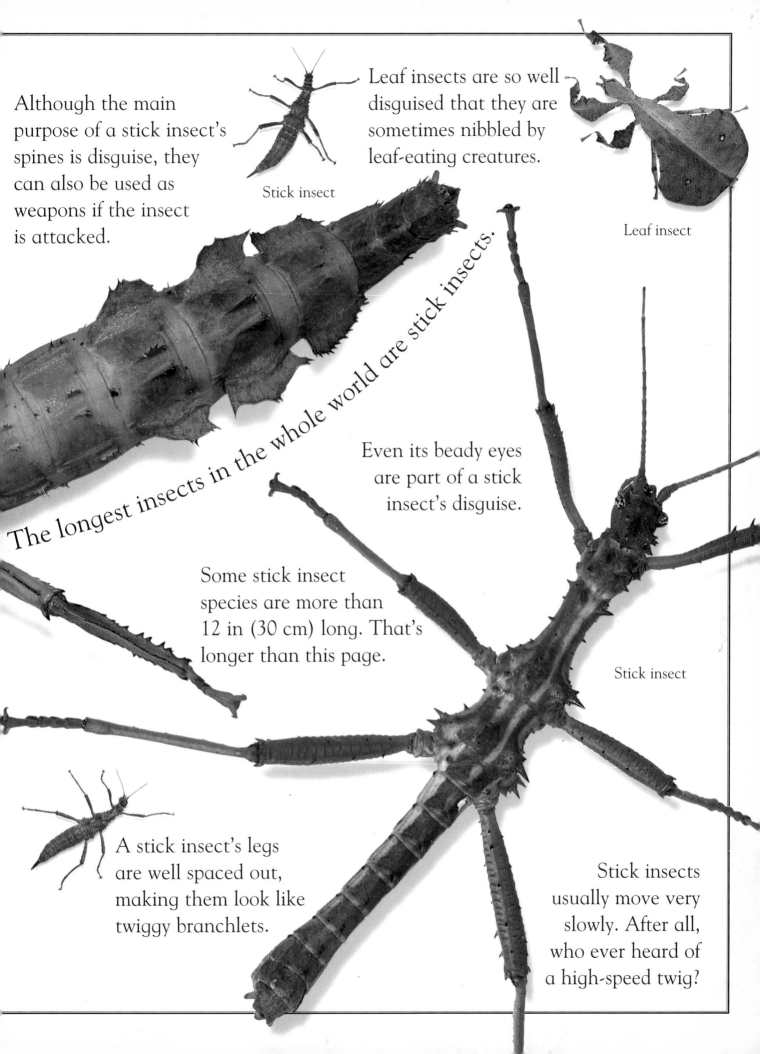

Although the main purpose of a stick insect's spines is disguise, they can also be used as weapons if the insect is attacked.

Stick insect

Leaf insects are so well disguised that they are sometimes nibbled by leaf-eating creatures.

Leaf insect

The longest insects in the whole world are stick insects.

Even its beady eyes are part of a stick insect's disguise.

Some stick insect species are more than 12 in (30 cm) long. That's longer than this page.

Stick insect

A stick insect's legs are well spaced out, making them look like twiggy branchlets.

Stick insects usually move very slowly. After all, who ever heard of a high-speed twig?

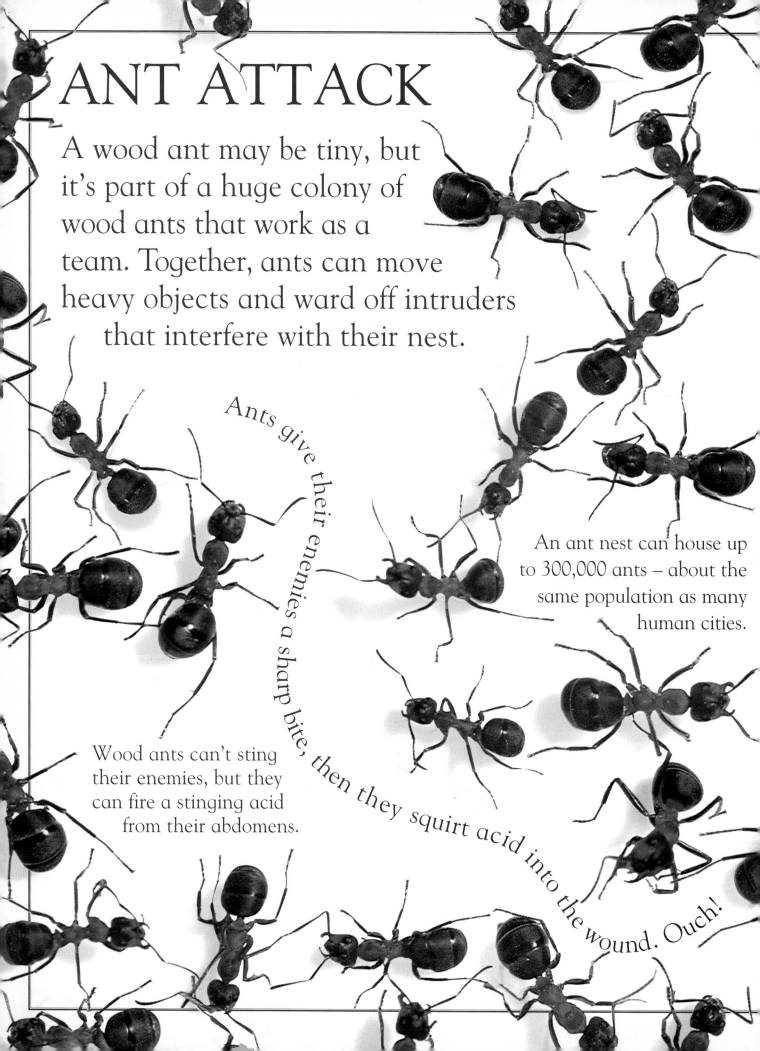

# ANT ATTACK

A wood ant may be tiny, but it's part of a huge colony of wood ants that work as a team. Together, ants can move heavy objects and ward off intruders that interfere with their nest.

Ants give their enemies a sharp bite, then they squirt acid into the wound. Ouch!

An ant nest can house up to 300,000 ants – about the same population as many human cities.

Wood ants can't sting their enemies, but they can fire a stinging acid from their abdomens.

When an ant finds a dead insect that's too big to carry, it gets others to help break it up and drag it back to the nest.

The food-gathering ants in a nest are called worker ants.

Wood ants help forests by eating leaf-eating insect larvae.

# TINY TANKS

There are more than 350,000 kinds of beetles – more than any other animal on Earth. Each species is different, but they all have tough wing cases and strong jaws for biting.

Rhinoceros beetle

Rove beetle

This rove beetle cuts up prey with its scissorlike jaws.

Rhinoceros beetles are the world's strongest animals, lifting 850 times their own weight. That's like you carrying 850 of your friends.

Well-armored male beetles do battle to impress females.

Minotaur beetle

Male minotaur beetles give presents of rabbit droppings to females. The females lay their eggs in the droppings.

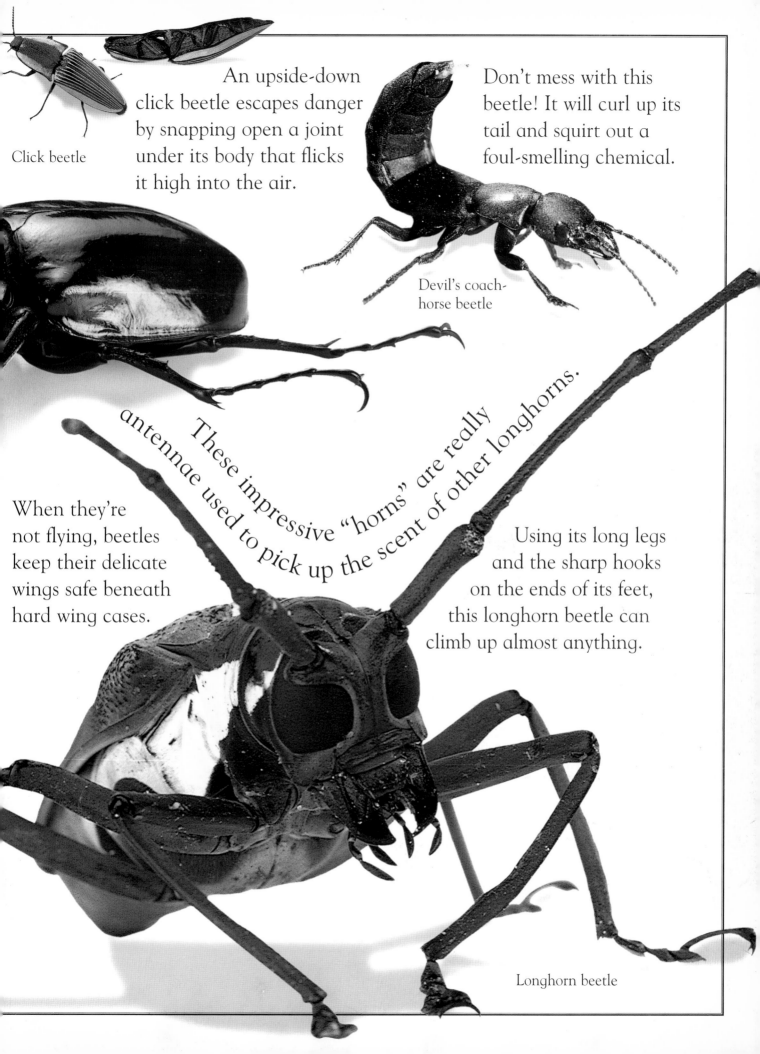

An upside-down click beetle escapes danger by snapping open a joint under its body that flicks it high into the air.

Click beetle

Don't mess with this beetle! It will curl up its tail and squirt out a foul-smelling chemical.

Devil's coach-horse beetle

These impressive "horns" are really antennae used to pick up the scent of other longhorns.

When they're not flying, beetles keep their delicate wings safe beneath hard wing cases.

Using its long legs and the sharp hooks on the ends of its feet, this longhorn beetle can climb up almost anything.

Longhorn beetle

# BEASTLY BUGS

All bugs have tube-shaped mouths designed for sucking liquids. Some live entirely on the sugary sap in plants, while others suck the fluids out of other insects or larger animals.

Shield bug

Some scientists think that this bug's strange-shaped head and big eyes help it scare away predators.

Shield bug

Bright colors warn predators that a bug tastes bad, while green helps it hide.

Shield bug

Shield bug

When a lantern bug is disturbed, it lets off a nasty smell, flashes its bright wings, and shakes its rattly head.

Assassin bugs snatch small insects, pierce them with their sharp mouthparts, and then suck out their juices.

Bedbug

Assassin bug

Shield bug

At night, bedbugs crawl out of warm, dark crevices to suck the blood of any people or animals sleeping nearby.

Shield bugs are also called stink bugs because they give off awful smells that can cause headaches.

Watch out in tropical rivers – this water bug is known as the "toe-biter."

Lantern bug

This bug hides in water weeds waiting to ambush small fish, tadpoles, and other tasty water creatures.

Water bug